INTRODUCTION

Why include team building activ breakers in your company

How to organize icebreakers and team-building activities more effectively

ADAPTING ICEBREAKERS TO YOUR TEAM SIZE

Warm-up activities for your small group or team

Activities for a big group or team

ACTIVITIES THAT HELP THE INTRODUCTION OF TEAM MEMBERS

ACTIVITIES THAT HELP PEOPLE WORK TOGETHER MORE EFFECTIVELY

ACTIVITIES THAT HELP PEOPLE WORK TOGETHER MORE EFFECTIVELY

Examples of team-building activities that help people work together more effectively

Examples of team-building activities that encourage problem solving

Examples of team-building activities that develop trust between team members

Activities that focus on improving verbal and nonverbal communication in the team

ACTIVITIES THAT AIM TO STIMULATE CREATIVITY AND INNOVATION IN THE TEAM

Warm-up activities for your small group or team

Activities for a big group or team

TABLE OF CONTENTS

ACTIVITIES THAT HELP REMOTE TEAM MEMBERS

Examples of team-building activities for remote teams
Activities that help remote team members to know each other better

ICEBREAKERS FOR VIRTUAL MEETINGS

Activities that help to energize and engage virtual meeting participants
Examples of Energizers for virtual meetings

ICEBREAKERS FOR REORGANIZING AND WELDING THE TEAM

Examples of icebreakers when a new team member joins the team
Icebreakers for a team with new leadership
Activities that help reorganize and welding the team
Icebreakers when a team has experienced conflict or tension

ICEBREAKERS FOR MULTICULTURAL TEAMS

ICEBREAKERS FOR DIFFERENT AGE GROUPS

ICEBREAKERS FOR DIFFERENT LOCATIONS

Icebreakers for outdoor company activities
Outdoor activities to enhance team creativity
Icebreakers for active teams at the pool or beach
Icebreakers for active teams at the mountains
Icebreakers for active teams in the snow/ winter

CARD GAME OR TRIVIA ICEBREAKERS

INTRODUCTION

Why include team building activities and ice breakers in your company

Ice breaker activities are often used in team-building and group-bonding exercises, as well as in training sessions and workshops.

Ice breaker activities are important for companies for a variety of reasons:

These activities help to build strong and cohesive teams, improve communication, increase productivity, and create a positive and inclusive work environment.

One of the main reasons for the importance of ice breaker activities is that they help to build strong and cohesive teams. These activities allow team members to get to know one another on a personal level, which can lead to better communication, trust, and understanding among team members. This can help to improve team dynamics and increase overall team performance.

Another reason for the importance of ice breaker activities is that they can help to improve communication among team members. By participating in these activities, team members are able to practice their communication skills in a safe and non-threatening environment. This can help to reduce communication barriers and increase the overall effectiveness of communication within the team.

Ice breaker activities can also help to increase productivity among team members. By participating in these activities, team members are able to take a break from their regular work tasks and engage in activities that are designed to help them relax and recharge. This can lead to increased motivation and engagement among team members, which can ultimately lead to increased productivity.

Ice breaker activities can also help to create a positive and inclusive work environment. These activities can help to break down barriers between team members and promote a sense of belonging and acceptance among team members. This can lead to a more positive and inclusive work culture, which can ultimately lead to increased employee satisfaction and retention.

In conclusion, ice breaker activities for companies are important for a variety of reasons. They help to build strong and cohesive teams, improve communication, increase productivity, and create a positive and inclusive work environment. By incorporating ice breaker activities into your company's culture, you can create a more positive and productive work environment for your employees.

How to organize icebreakers and team-building activities more effectively

Set clear objectives: Determine the goals of the activity, such as improving teamwork, problem-solving, or communication skills, and make sure that the activity is tailored to achieve those goals.

Create a plan: Plan the activity in advance, including the materials and resources needed, the timeline, and the instructions for participants.

Assign roles: Assign roles to participants, such as team leader, timekeeper, or facilitator, to ensure that the activity runs smoothly.

Tailor the activity to the group: Consider the size of the group, their backgrounds, and their skill levels when selecting the activity.

Provide instructions and guidelines: Clearly explain the instructions and guidelines for the activity, and make sure that all participants understand what is expected of them.

Monitor and debrief: Monitor the activity and debrief after it's done, to discuss the outcome, what worked well and what could be improved.

Encourage participation: Encourage all participants to participate and contribute to the activity, and create a supportive and inclusive environment.

Provide feedback: Provide feedback to participants on their performance, and offer suggestions for improvement.

Use a variety of activities: Use a variety of activities to keep things interesting and engaging, and to target different skills and objectives.

Follow up: Follow up with the group after the activity to see if the objectives were met and if the team has improved in the targeted areas.

ADAPTING ICEBREAKERS TO YOUR TEAM SIZE

Adapting icebreakers to team size is crucial for the success of the activity. A team of 50 people will have different needs and dynamics than a team of 5. Here are some tips for adapting icebreakers to team size:

Break the team into smaller groups: For larger teams, it can be difficult for everyone to participate in the same activity. Breaking the team into smaller groups allows for more personalized and intimate interactions.

Use technology: For remote teams or large teams, technology can be a useful tool for conducting icebreakers. Virtual icebreakers can be done through video conferencing software and can be a great way to connect with team members who are working from different locations.

Focus on communication: Large teams may have different communication styles and needs. Icebreakers that focus on communication can help team members understand and appreciate different perspectives.

Be mindful of time: Large teams may have limited time for icebreakers, so it's important to choose activities that can be completed in a short amount of time.

Customize the activity: It's important to tailor the activity to the specific needs and goals of the team. For example, if the team is working on a project that requires collaboration, choose an icebreaker that focuses on teamwork.

Keep it simple: With large teams, it can be easy to get bogged down in details. Keep the icebreaker simple and easy to understand so that everyone can participate.

Make it fun and engaging: Icebreakers should be enjoyable for everyone. Choose activities that are interactive, engaging and make team members feel comfortable.

Use a facilitator: A facilitator can help keep the icebreaker on track, answer questions, and provide guidance to participants.

In conclusion, adapting icebreakers to team size requires careful consideration of the team dynamics, the goals of the icebreaker and the time available. By breaking the team into smaller groups, using technology, focusing on communication, customizing the activity, keeping it simple, making it fun and engaging and using a facilitator, you can make sure that the icebreaker is effective and enjoyable for all team members.

Warm-up activities for your small group or team:

Warm-up activities can be a great way to get a small group or team energized and ready to work together. Here are some examples of warm-up activities that can be used to kick off a meeting or team-building session:

"Two Truths and a Lie" where each person shares two facts about themselves and one lie, and the group has to guess which statement is the lie.

"Name Game" where each person shares their name and something they like, and the group has to repeat all of the names and likes in order.

"Word Association" where one person starts with a word and the next person has to say a word that's associated with it.

"Energy Ball" where team members pass a ball around the circle while saying their name and an adjective that describes their energy level.

"Human Knot" where team members stand in a circle, hold hands with someone who is not next to them, and then try to untangle themselves without letting go.

"Energizer Scavenger Hunt" where team members search the room for hidden items that correspond with different energizer activities.

"Morning Check-in" where team members share their mood and what they're looking forward to that day.

"Emoji Game" where team members describe a word or phrase using only emoji.

"Trust Walk" where participants are blindfolded and led by a partner through a course.

"Group Juggle" where team members pass around a small object and try to keep it in the air as long as possible.

"Circle of Trust" where participants stand in a circle and take turns falling back into the arms of the group, building trust.

"Roll Call" where participants say their name and a funny fact about themselves

These activities can help team members to bond and get to know each other better, while also helping to create a positive and energized environment. It's important to choose activities that are appropriate for the group's level of familiarity, culture and backgrounds.

Activities for a big group or team

Here are some examples of activities that can be used to kick off a meeting or team-building session:

"Stand-up, Sit-down" where team members stand up when a certain phrase is said, and sit down when another phrase is said.
"Team Building Puzzle" where team members have to put together a puzzle as a group
"Trust Walk" where team members have to walk blindfolded and rely on the instructions of their teammates
"Group Storytelling" where team members take turns adding to a story as a group
"Team Building Relay Race" where team members have to complete a series of tasks as a group
"Group Yoga" where team members do yoga exercises together

"Team Building Treasure Hunt" where team members have to work together to find hidden treasure

"Group Charades" where team members act out words or phrases as a group
"Team Building Escape Room" where team members have to work together to solve puzzles and escape a themed room
"Group Improvisation" where team members have to act out a scenario on the spot with no pre-planning
"Team Building Scavenger Hunt" where team members have to work together to find a list of items.
"Energizer Dance" where participants stand in a circle and do a group dance to a song that gets everyone moving.

"Line Up" where participants have to line up in order based on specific criteria, such as birthdays or shoe size.

"Team Mascot" where participants create a team mascot and a cheer for that mascot

"Pass the Message" where participants pass a message verbally through the group

"Human Word Chain" where participants have to say a word that's related to a previous word

"Team Cheer" where participants create a unique cheer or chant for their team.

"Team Introductions" where participants introduce teams and their role in company

"The Storyteller" where participants have to tell a story with a specific theme or keyword

These activities can help team members to bond and get to know each other better, while also helping to create a positive and energized environment. It's important to choose activities that are appropriate for the group's level of familiarity, culture and backgrounds.

Line Up

"Line Up" is a warm-up activity that can help a large group of people get to know each other better and also helps to break the ice. The activity is simple to set up and can be customized to suit the group's needs.

Example:

The group stands in a circle, facing each other.

The facilitator gives a specific criteria for the group to line up by, such as birthdays, shoe size, or favorite color.
Participants must quickly find their place in the line based on the given criteria.
Once the line is formed, participants can introduce themselves to those around them.
The facilitator can also ask questions to the group, such as "Why did you choose to stand where you are?" or "What did you learn about the person next to you?"

This activity can also be modified with different criteria or teams and can be used as a warm-up activity or a team-building activity.

Team Building Puzzle

"Team Building Puzzle" is a game that aims to promote teamwork and problem-solving skills among team members. The game is played by dividing the team into smaller groups and giving each group a set of puzzle pieces. The goal of the game is for each group to work together to assemble the puzzle as quickly as possible.
Example:
- Divide the team into groups of 4-6 people
- Give each group a set of puzzle pieces and a picture of the finished puzzle
- Set a timer for 30 minutes
- The group that finishes the puzzle first wins a prize
- After the game, have a debriefing session to discuss the teamwork and communication skills used during the game and how they can be applied to the team's work.

This game is a good icebreaker for a team with new leadership as it promotes communication and collaboration among team members, and it allows the new leader to observe the dynamics of the team and identify areas for improvement. Additionally, it's a great way to introduce new team members, and get the team bonding and working together.

EXAMPLES OF ACTIVITIES THAT HELP THE INTRODUCTION OF TEAM MEMBERS

Introductions activities are typically used at the beginning of a new team or group forming, such as at the start of a new project or at the beginning of a new work term. These activities help people to get to know each other's names, backgrounds, and interests, which can help to build a sense of camaraderie and teamwork.

Additionally, these activities can also help to break the ice and reduce any initial tension or awkwardness that may exist among group members. It is also a good idea to use these activities when new members join the team, as it will help them to integrate more easily into the group.

Overall, these activities are a great way to start any team-building or training session, and to create a more cohesive and effective team.

Examples of activities

Two Truths and a Lie: Participants introduce themselves by sharing two true facts about themselves and one false fact, and the group has to guess which one is the lie.

Name Tags: Participants create name tags with interesting facts or hobbies written on them, and wear them throughout the event.

Speed Networking: Participants engage in quick, informal conversations with different people to learn more about each other's backgrounds and interests.

Name Game: Participants form a circle and take turns saying their name and an interesting fact or hobby, with the goal of remembering everyone's name by the end.

Show and Tell: Participants bring in an object that represents them and talk about why it's meaningful to them, giving others a glimpse into their background and interests.

Trivia Challenge: Participants form teams and compete against each other in a trivia game based on each other's backgrounds and interests.

Icebreaker Roulette: Participants will be randomly matched with a colleague and have to interview each other to learn more about their background, interests, and goals.

Who Am I: Participants are given a sheet of paper with a famous person's name written on it, and have to ask yes or no questions to figure out who they are supposed to be.

My Life in Pictures: Participants bring in a few pictures from their life and share the story behind each one, giving others a sense of their background and interests.

Team Building Scavenger Hunt: Participants are divided into teams and have to work together to complete a scavenger hunt that includes questions about each other's backgrounds and interests.

Show and Tell

"Show and Tell" is a simple and effective icebreaker activity that can be used to introduce a new team member, or to help team members get to know each other better. The activity involves each team member bringing an object or item that represents something about themselves or their interests, and then sharing it with the group. The object can be something personal, such as a photograph or a trinket, or it can be something related to their work, such as a tool or piece of equipment.

Example:
1. Each team member is asked to bring an object or item that represents something about themselves or their interests to the next team meeting.
2. During the meeting, each team member takes turns sharing their object or item with the group, and explaining why it is meaningful to them.
3. Team members can ask questions or share their own related experiences.
4. The activity can also be adapted by adding a guessing game where team members try to guess which team member brought which object and why it is meaningful to them.
5. This activity can be used to help team members get to know each other better and to encourage open communication and trust within the team. It can also be a good way to break the ice and make the team more comfortable with each other.

TEAM BUILDING ACTIVITIES THAT HELP PEOPLE WORK TOGETHER MORE EFFECTIVELY

Activities that help people work together more effectively can be used in a variety of situations, such as:

When a new team is formed and team members need to get to know each other and establish trust

When a team is experiencing conflicts or tension, and team members need to work on communication and collaboration skills

When a team is feeling disengaged or unmotivated, and team members need to be re-energized and re-engaged

When a team is working on a new project or initiative and needs to brainstorm and generate new ideas

When a team is facing a difficult challenge or problem and needs to improve problem-solving and decision-making skills

When a team is working remotely and needs to build stronger connections and improve communication among team members.

Problem-solving, communication, and trust exercises should be used when a team is working on a project or task that requires collaboration and cooperation. These activities can help team members learn how to communicate effectively, work together efficiently, and build trust with one another. They can be especially useful when a team is struggling with conflicts or tension, or when new team members are joining the team and need to learn how to work with others. Additionally, these activities can be used as a way to improve the overall performance of a team, by helping them to identify and address any issues that may be hindering their productivity or success.

Examples of team-building activities that help people work together more effectively:

The Marshmallow Challenge: Participants work in teams to build the tallest structure possible using only marshmallows and toothpicks, with the goal of fostering problem-solving and teamwork skills.

The Blindfolded Puzzle: Participants work in teams to complete a puzzle while blindfolded, with the goal of developing trust and communication skills.

The Human Knot: Participants stand in a circle, hold hands with someone they don't know, and then work together to unravel the "knot" without letting go of each other's hands.

The Tower of Tissues: Participants work in teams to build the tallest tower possible using only tissues, with the goal of promoting teamwork and problem-solving skills.

The Egg Drop: Participants work in teams to design and build a container that will protect an egg from breaking when dropped from a height, with the goal of fostering creativity, problem-solving, and teamwork.

Escape Room: Participants work together to solve a series of clues and puzzles in order to escape a room, promoting problem-solving, teamwork, and communication skills.

The Communication Game: Participants will be placed in a challenging situation where they have to communicate effectively to achieve a common goal.

The Minefield: Participants have to navigate through a minefield blindfolded, using verbal instructions from their teammates to avoid the "mines".

The Marshmallow Challenge: Participants work in teams to build the tallest structure possible using only marshmallows and toothpicks, with the goal of fostering problem-solving and teamwork skills.

The Blindfolded Puzzle: Participants work in teams to complete a puzzle while blindfolded, with the goal of developing trust and communication skills.

The Human Knot: Participants stand in a circle, hold hands with someone they don't know, and then work together to unravel the "knot" without letting go of each other's hands.

The Tower of Tissues: Participants work in teams to build the tallest tower possible using only tissues, with the goal of promoting teamwork and problem-solving skills.

The Egg Drop: Participants work in teams to design and build a container that will protect an egg from breaking when dropped from a height, with the goal of fostering creativity, problem-solving, and teamwork.

Escape Room: Participants work together to solve a series of clues and puzzles in order to escape a room, promoting problem-solving, teamwork, and communication skills.

The Communication Game: Participants will be placed in a challenging situation where they have to communicate effectively to achieve a common goal.

The Minefield: Participants have to navigate through a minefield blindfolded, using verbal instructions from their teammates to avoid the "mines".

Examples of team-building activities that encourage problem solving:

The Human Knot is a team-building activity that helps to promote communication, trust, and problem-solving skills. The activity involves a group of people standing in a circle and holding hands with people who are not next to them. The group then must work together to untangle themselves without letting go of each other's hands.

Example:
- A group of 10 people are participating in the activity.
- They are instructed to stand in a circle and hold hands with people who are not next to them.
- The group will then start to move and communicate to untangle themselves without letting go of each other's hands.
- They may take different strategies, like, forming smaller sub-groups, creating a chain to move around the circle, or working with the people they are holding hands with.
- Once they have successfully untangled themselves, they will reflect on the experience and discuss how they worked together, what communication strategies they used, and how they overcame any challenges they encountered.

This activity can be adapted to suit different group sizes and can be modified to incorporate specific goals or learning objectives. Additionally, it can be used as an icebreaker for a new team, or as a way to help a team that is experiencing conflict or tension to work through their issues and improve their communication and collaboration skills.

The Minefield: Participants have to navigate through a minefield blindfolded, using verbal instructions from their teammates to avoid the "mines", it will encourage problem solving.

The Human Bridge: Participants have to work together to build a bridge using only their bodies, to cross over an obstacle.

The Amazing Race: Participants work in teams to complete a series of challenges and puzzles at different locations, promoting problem-solving and teamwork skills.

The Decision-Making Challenge: Participants work in teams to evaluate different options and make a decision based on a simulated scenario, promoting problem-solving and critical thinking skills.

Here is an example of a Decision-Making Challenge game:

Objective: To improve problem-solving and critical thinking skills among team members.

Instructions:

Divide the group into teams of 4-6 people.

Provide each team with a scenario that requires a decision to be made. The scenario could be based on a hypothetical business or real-life situation.

Give the teams a set amount of time to discuss and evaluate different options.

Have each team present their decision and the reasoning behind it to the rest of the group.

Facilitate a group discussion to evaluate the decision-making process and the outcome.

Provide feedback on the team's decision-making skills and offer suggestions for improvement.

Scenario: Your team is a group of consultants hired by a company to help them increase their market share. The company is considering launching a new product, but they are not sure which product would be the most successful. The team must decide which product to launch based on the information provided.

Example options:

A line of eco-friendly cleaning products

A line of organic, non-GMO snacks

A line of energy-efficient appliances

The teams will have to use their critical thinking and problem solving skills to evaluate the options, and make a decision based on the information provided. The decision will then be discussed and evaluated with the rest of the group, providing feedback to the team on the skills used and areas for improvement.

Examples of team-building activities that develop trust between team members

The Blindfold Walk: Participants are blindfolded and have to rely on their teammates to guide them through an obstacle course, promoting trust and communication skills.

The Trust Fall: Participants stand at the edge of a platform and fall backwards, trusting their teammates to catch them.

The Human Ladder: Participants have to trust their teammates to support them as they climb over a wall or other obstacle.

The Trust Walk: Participants are blindfolded and have to rely on their teammates to guide them through an obstacle course, promoting trust and communication skills.

The Tightrope Walk: Participants have to trust their teammates to steady them as they walk across a tightrope.

The Trust Circle: Participants stand in a circle and have to catch one another as they fall, promoting trust and teamwork.

The Trust Walk: Participants are blindfolded and have to rely on their teammates to guide them through an obstacle course, promoting trust and communication skills.

The Human Knot: Participants stand in a circle, hold hands with someone they don't know, and then work together to unravel the "knot" without letting go of each other's hands.

The Trust Fall: Participants stand at the edge of a platform and fall backwards, trusting their teammates to catch them.

The Trust Tower: Participants have to work together to build a tower using only their bodies, promoting trust and teamwork.

Activities that focus on improving verbal and nonverbal communication in the team

The Communication Scavenger Hunt: Participants work in teams to find and collect specific items, practicing verbal and nonverbal communication skills as they interact with one another and complete the task.

The Telephone Game: Participants sit in a circle and pass a message around by whispering, highlighting the importance of clear communication and the impact of misinterpretation.

Charades: Participants act out words or phrases without speaking, highlighting the importance of nonverbal communication.

The Body Language Game: Participants have to interpret the body language of their teammates and guess what they're thinking or feeling, practicing observation and interpretation of nonverbal cues.

The Debate Game: Participants have to debate a topic in a team, highlighting the importance of verbal communication, active listening and effective argumentation.

The Wordless Meeting: Participants conduct a meeting without speaking, using only nonverbal cues to communicate, highlighting the importance of nonverbal communication.

The Listening Game: Participants take turns talking while the others focus on active listening, highlighting the importance of effective listening skills.

The Empathy Game: Participants put themselves in the shoes of another person, and have to communicate their thoughts and feelings, highlighting the importance of effective empathy and verbal communication.

The Mirror Game: Participants take turns mimicking the actions of their partner, highlighting the importance of nonverbal communication and observation skills.

The Communication Mixer: Participants are given a conversation starter, and have to talk to different people while practicing effective verbal and nonverbal communication skills.

ACTIVITIES THAT AIM TO STIMULATE CREATIVITY AND INNOVATION IN THE TEAM

Creativity is useful for a company because it allows for the development of new and innovative ideas and solutions. This can lead to increased productivity, efficiency, and competitiveness within the market. Additionally, fostering a culture of creativity can also lead to increased job satisfaction and employee engagement, which can result in lower turnover rates and higher levels of employee retention. Creativity can also lead to the development of new products, services, and revenue streams for a company, providing a source of growth and expansion. In addition, encouraging creativity can also lead to more diverse perspectives and ideas within a team, which can promote more inclusive and effective decision-making.

Activities that aim to stimulate creativity and innovation in the team are best used when a team shows limitations, lack of enthusiasm and at the beginning of a new project, a new season, etc. Additionally, these activities may be useful when a company wants to encourage employees to think outside the box and come up with new ideas for their product or service.

Examples of team-building activities that encourage people to think outside the box and come up with new ideas

The Mind Map: Participants work individually or in teams to create a visual representation of their ideas, using colors, images, and words to explore new possibilities.

The Brainstorming Game: Participants work in teams to generate as many ideas as possible within a set timeframe, using a variety of techniques such as free association and random word triggers.

The Reverse Brainstorming: Participants work in teams to generate ideas for the opposite of a given problem or goal, encouraging them to think creatively and outside of their usual frame of reference.

The Random Word Game: Participants are given a random word and have to come up with as many creative uses for it as possible.

The Idea Shuffle: Participants work in teams to combine different ideas or concepts to create something new, encouraging them to think outside of the box.

The Puzzle Challenge: Participants have to solve a puzzle or riddle that requires creative thinking and out-of-the-box problem-solving skills.

The Innovation Game: Participants work in teams to come up with new ideas or improve existing products or processes, encouraging them to think creatively and outside of their usual frame of reference.

The Role-playing Scenario: Participants act out different scenarios and have to come up with new and creative solutions to the problems that arise, encouraging them to think outside the box.

The Picture Puzzle: Participants are shown a picture and have to come up with as many different story ideas or interpretations as possible.

The Random Object Game: Participants are given a random object and have to come up with as many different uses for it as possible, encouraging out-of-the-box thinking.

Innovation Game

The Innovation Game is a team building exercise that encourages people to think creatively and come up with new ideas. Here is an example of how it can be run:

Divide the group into teams of 3-5 people.

Give each team a problem or challenge that they need to solve. This could be something related to the company's products or processes, or a more general problem that is relevant to the group's work.

Give the teams a set amount of time (such as 1 hour) to brainstorm and come up with as many ideas as possible.

After the brainstorming session, have each team present their ideas to the group. Encourage open and honest feedback, and ask for suggestions for improvement.

After all the teams have presented, have the group vote on the best idea. The team that came up with the winning idea gets a prize (it could be a small gift, a certificate or a token).

Finally, encourage the teams to continue working on their ideas in order to implement them.

This activity can be run periodically to keep the team's innovative thinking skills sharp and to encourage them to think outside of their usual frame of reference.

The Picture Puzzle

The Picture Puzzle is a team building exercise that encourages people to think creatively and come up with new ideas. Here is an example of how it can be run:

Divide the group into teams of 3-5 people.
Show the teams a picture, it could be an abstract image or a photograph that depict a particular scene or an object.
Give each team a set amount of time (such as 20 minutes) to come up with as many different story ideas or interpretations of the picture as possible.
After the brainstorming session, have each team present their ideas to the group. Encourage open and honest feedback, and ask for suggestions for improvement.
After all the teams have presented, have the group vote on the best story idea. The team that came up with the winning idea gets a prize (it could be a small gift, a certificate or a token).
Finally, encourage the teams to continue working on their story ideas and develop them further, this could be done as a writing exercise or a role-playing scenario.
This activity can be run periodically to keep the team's creative thinking skills sharp and
 to encourage them to think outside of their usual frame of reference.

Innovation Game

The Idea Shuffle is an icebreaker game that can be used to stimulate creativity and innovation within a team. The game is designed to generate a large number of ideas in a short amount of time and encourages team members to think outside of the box.

Example:
- Divide the team into small groups of about 4-5 people each.
- Give each group a blank sheet of paper and a pen.
- Set a timer for 10-15 minutes and ask the groups to brainstorm as many ideas as they can related to a specific topic (e.g. how to improve customer service, how to increase sales, etc.).
- Once the timer goes off, have each group present their ideas to the whole team.
- Next, ask the team to take all the ideas generated by all the groups and shuffle them up.
- Then, divide the team into new groups, and give each group a set of the ideas generated by all the teams.
- Ask each group to select the top 5 ideas from the set and present them to the whole team.
- Finally, have the team select the best idea and work on implementing it.

This game allows team members to share their thoughts and ideas and encourages collaboration and creativity. It can be a fun and engaging way to come up with new solutions to problems or identify new opportunities for the team.

ACTIVITIES THAT HELP REMOTE TEAM MEMBERS

Team building is needed in a remote team of a company for several reasons:

Building trust and relationships: Remote teams often lack the opportunity to build personal connections and trust through face-to-face interactions. Team building activities can help remote team members get to know each other better and build stronger working relationships.

Improving communication: Remote teams often struggle with communication, and team building activities can help team members learn how to communicate more effectively with each other.

Enhancing collaboration: Remote teams can have difficulty collaborating and working together effectively. Team building activities can help remote team members learn how to work together more efficiently and productively.

Boosting motivation and engagement: Remote teams can feel isolated and disconnected, which can lead to low motivation and engagement. Team building activities can help re-energize and re-engage team members.

Fostering creativity and innovation: Remote teams may lack the opportunity to brainstorm and collaborate in person, which can stifle creativity and innovation. Team building activities can help remote teams generate new ideas and solve problems more effectively.

Improving team performance: By addressing the challenges and opportunities of remote teams, team building activities can ultimately improve team performance and productivity.

Examples of team-building activities for remote teams

Virtual Icebreakers: Host a virtual meeting to introduce team members, share interests and hobbies, and play interactive games to get to know each other.

Virtual Team-Building Activities: Use virtual tools to facilitate team-building exercises such as problem-solving challenges and communication exercises.

Virtual Social Hours: Set up regular virtual social hours for team members to connect informally and chat about non-work related topics.

Virtual Book Club: Start a virtual book club where team members can discuss a chosen book, share their thoughts and ideas, and connect with each other.

Virtual Game Night: Organize a virtual game night where team members can play games together, such as online trivia or virtual escape rooms.

Virtual Team-Building Retreat: Host a virtual team-building retreat, where team members can participate in activities such as yoga, meditation, and mindfulness exercises.

Virtual Volunteer Opportunities: Organize virtual volunteer opportunities for team members to give back to the community and bond over a shared cause.

Virtual Team-Building Challenges: Set up virtual team-building challenges, such as a fitness challenge or a cooking challenge, to encourage team members to bond and connect over a shared goal.

Virtual Movie Night: Host a virtual movie night where team members can watch a movie together and discuss it afterwards, fostering a sense of connection and camaraderie.

Virtual Team-Building Classes: Organize virtual team-building classes, such as language classes or cooking classes, to encourage team members to learn new skills and connect over a shared interest.

Activities that help remote team members to know each other better

Virtual Introductions: Host a virtual meeting to introduce team members and have them share a bit about themselves, such as their background, interests, and hobbies.
Virtual "Show and Tell": Have team members share something from their home office or personal life during a virtual meeting, to give others a glimpse into their personal lives and interests.
Virtual "Two Truths and a Lie": Host a virtual game where team members share three statements about themselves, two of
which are true and one of which is a lie, and have the group guess which statement is the lie.
Virtual "Speed Friending": Set up virtual "speed friending" sessions, where team members have short, one-on-one conversations with different team members to get to know them better.
Virtual "Share Your Story": Encourage team members to share their personal stories, such as their career journey or a defining moment in their life, during a virtual meeting.
Virtual "Team Trivia": Host a virtual trivia game where team members can showcase their knowledge of each other's backgrounds, interests, and hobbies.

Virtual "Team Scavenger Hunt": Create a virtual scavenger hunt where team members have to find information about their colleagues to complete the challenge.

Virtual "Who Am I?" game: Host a virtual game where team members have to guess the identity of their colleagues based on a few clues or personal characteristics

Virtual "Get to know" Session: schedule regular virtual "get to know" sessions where team members can share information about their interests, hobbies, and personal lives, fostering connection and camaraderie.

Virtual "Team Building" activities: Organize virtual team building activities that encourage team members to learn more about each other, such as virtual escape rooms, virtual treasure hunts, or virtual scavenger hunts.

Example: Virtual "Team Scavenger Hunt"

Objective: To encourage team members to get to know each other better and to foster a sense of connection and camaraderie among the team.

Instructions:

Divide the team into groups of 3-4 people.

Provide each group with a list of items or information that they need to find out about their team members (e.g. their favorite color, their favorite movie, their favorite hobby, etc.)

Set a time limit for the scavenger hunt (e.g. 30 minutes).

During the scavenger hunt, team members can use virtual communication tools such as video conferencing or instant messaging to collaborate and find the information they need.

At the end of the scavenger hunt, have each group present the information they have gathered about their team members to the rest of the team.

reward the winning group with a prize (e.g. a virtual gift card)

This activity is a fun way to encourage team members to get to know each other better and to foster a sense of connection and camaraderie among the team. It also allows team members to use and improve their communication skills, problem-solving skills, and teamwork skills.

Example: Virtual "Speed Friending"

Objective: To encourage team members to get to know each other better and to foster a sense of connection and camaraderie among the team.

Instructions:

Set up a virtual meeting platform (e.g. Zoom, Google Meet) for the "speed friending" session.

Divide the team into pairs or small groups.

Set a time limit for each "speed friending" session (e.g. 5-10 minutes per pair/group).

During the "speed friending" session, team members should take turns introducing themselves and asking each other questions about their background, interests, and hobbies.

After each "speed friending" session, team members should switch partners or groups, to meet and talk with different team members.

Repeat the process for the set time limit, so that team members can meet and talk with as many team members as possible.

This activity is a fun and efficient way to encourage team members to get to know each other better and to foster a sense of connection and camaraderie among the team. It also allows team members to improve their communication skills and interpersonal skills, as they will have to introduce themselves and engage in conversations with different team members.

Example: Virtual "Show and Tell"

The Virtual "Show and Tell" activity is a great way to get to know your team members and to break the ice when working remotely. The activity can be done via video conferencing or chat.

Example:
1. Set a time for the virtual "Show and Tell" session.
2. Each team member should prepare an object that represents something about themselves (e.g. a hobby, an interesting fact, a favorite book, etc.).
3. During the session, each team member will have a few minutes to show their object and talk about what it represents.
4. Encourage team members to ask questions and interact with each other during the session.
5. After the activity, have a group discussion about what was learned and how it can help improve teamwork.

This activity is a great way to build trust, communication, and understanding among team members. It can also help team members to remember each other's names, backgrounds, and interests, which can be helpful when working together in the future.

ICEBREAKERS FOR VIRTUAL MEETINGS

Virtual "Virtual Escape Room": Participants are given a theme, and have to use their problem-solving skills to escape a virtual escape room by solving puzzles and riddles.

Activities that help to energize and engage virtual meeting participants:

Virtual "Icebreaker Bingo": Create a bingo board with different icebreaker questions or prompts (e.g. "Has been to more than 5 countries," "Has a pet," "Has a hobby that starts with the letter 'P'," etc.). Participants can fill in their bingo board during the meeting and share their answers with the group.

Virtual "Two Truths and a Lie": Each participant shares three statements about themselves, two of which are true and one of which is a lie. The other participants try to guess which statement is the lie.

Virtual "Show and Tell": Participants can share something from their home office or work space, or something personal that represents them.

Virtual "Emoji Story": Participants use emojis to create a story and present it to the group.

Virtual "Word Association": Participants take turns saying a word and the next participant has to say a word that is associated with the previous word.

Virtual "Virtual Tour": Participants take turns showing the group a virtual tour of their home or work environment, highlighting interesting features or personal touches.

Virtual "Virtual Selfie Scavenger Hunt": Participants are given a list of items to find and take a selfie with, such as a plant, a book, or a piece of art.

Virtual "Virtual Trivia": Participants compete in a trivia game related to their company, industry, or common interests.

Virtual "Virtual Escape Room": Participants are given a theme, and have to use their problem-solving skills to escape a virtual escape room by solving puzzles and riddles.

Examples of Energizers for virtual meetings

Energizers for virtual meetings are short activities or exercises that are designed to break up the monotony of long online meetings and keep participants engaged and focused. Here are a few examples:

1. "Virtual Scavenger Hunt": Participants are given a list of items to find within a set time limit, such as a pen and paper, a plant, or a picture of a pet.
2. "Virtual Escape Room": Participants work together to solve puzzles and clues in order to "escape" from a virtual room.
3. "Virtual Word Association": Participants take turns saying a word, and the next person has to say a word that is associated with the previous word.
4. "Virtual Charades": Participants act out different words or phrases for their team to guess.
5. "Virtual Yoga Break": Participants take a short break to do some simple yoga stretches, guided by an instructor via video conference.
6. "Virtual Team Building Game": Participants take part in a virtual team-building game that helps them collaborate and work together to achieve a common goal.
7. "Virtual Art Gallery": Participants share pictures of their favorite artworks and discuss their preferences.
8. "Virtual Music Break": Participants share their favorite songs and listen to them together during a break.
9. "Virtual Group Discussion": Participants are divided into small groups to discuss a given topic for a certain period of time, then come back to share their ideas with the whole team.

Virtual "Emoji Story"

A virtual "Emoji Story" icebreaker activity can be done through a video conferencing platform such as Zoom or Microsoft Teams. The activity can be used to encourage team members to think creatively and to get to know each other better. Here's an example of how the activity can be run:
1. Divide the team into small groups of 4-5 people.
2. Assign a leader for each group who will be responsible for keeping the conversation going and making sure everyone has a chance to participate.
3. Give each group a set of emojis (can be found online) and a scenario (e.g. "a day in the life of a team member" or "a company project gone wrong").
4. Each group must use the emojis to create a story that relates to the scenario.
5. Set a time limit for the activity (e.g. 20 minutes).
6. After the time is up, each group presents their story to the rest of the team.
7. Encourage the team to ask questions and give feedback on each group's story.

This activity is a great way to break the ice and promote creativity within the team. It also encourages team members to think outside the box and to work together to come up with a creative solution.

"Virtual Art Gallery"

"Virtual Art Gallery" is a virtual team building game that can be used to energize and engage participants during virtual meetings. The game is simple to set up and can be played on any video conferencing platform.
Here is an example of how to play the game:
1. Each team member selects a piece of art that they admire or that has meaning to them. It could be a painting, sculpture, photograph or any other type of art.
2. Each team member shares their chosen piece of art with the group and explains why they selected it. This could be done through a presentation or by sharing a photo of the art.
3. After everyone has shared their art, the team members can discuss their choices, share their thoughts and try to guess which artworks belong to each team member.
4. As an extension, team members can also create their own piece of art based on a theme or challenge set by the facilitator and share it with the group.

This game allows team members to learn more about each other's interests and tastes, as well as to think creatively. It also encourages team members to share their own personal insights, which can help to break down barriers and build stronger connections among team members.

"Virtual Word Association"

"Virtual Word Association" is a simple icebreaker game that can be played in a virtual meeting setting. The game works by having participants brainstorm a list of words related to a chosen theme, such as "teamwork" or "innovation."

Each participant takes turns sharing one word, and the rest of the team has to come up with another word that is related to the previous one. The goal is to see how creative and collaborative the team can be. For example, if the first word shared is "communication," the next word might be "listening," followed by "feedback," "understanding," "clarity," etc. This game can be used to break the ice and get people thinking creatively before diving into a more in-depth discussion or brainstorming session.

ICEBREAKERS FOR REORGANIZING AND WELDING THE TEAM

Icebreakers are important for reorganizing and welding a team for several reasons.

First and foremost, icebreakers help to break down barriers and facilitate communication among team members. In a newly formed or reorganized team, individuals may not know each other well, or may have different working styles, communication preferences, and backgrounds. Icebreakers can help team members get to know each other on a personal level and establish common ground, making it easier for them to work together effectively.

Second, icebreakers can also help to build trust and a sense of cohesion within the team. When team members participate in fun and interactive activities together, they are more likely to feel connected to one another and to the team as a whole. This can lead to increased motivation, productivity and a sense of belonging.

Examples of icebreakers when a new team member joins the team

"Two Truths and a Lie": Each team member shares three statements about themselves, and the rest of the team has to guess which one is a lie.

"Get to Know You" Bingo: Team members fill out a bingo card with their interests, hobbies, and background information, and then try to find others on the team who match the criteria.

"Name That Song": Team members take turns playing a few seconds of a song and the rest of the team has to guess the title and artist.

"Virtual Tour of My Space": The new team member shares a virtual tour of their home or office space.

"First Job": Team members share stories about their first job and what they learned from it.

"My Favorite Thing": Team members share their favorite book, movie, TV show, etc. and why they like it.

"Show and Tell": Team members bring in an item from home that holds special significance to them and share the story behind it.

"Icebreaker Questions": Team members take turns answering a set of pre-determined questions about themselves.

"The Name Game" - team members introduce themselves and share a fun fact or interesting hobby.

"The Interview Game" - team members take turns interviewing the new team member and learning about their background and experience.

"The Puzzle Challenge" - team members work together to complete a puzzle while getting to know the new team member.

"The Scavenger Hunt" - team members work together to find items that relate to the new team member's interests and background.

"The Speed Friending" - team members take turns talking to the new team member for a set amount of time, allowing them to quickly get to know each other.

"The Group Photo Challenge" - team members work together to take a group photo and get to know the new team member in the process.

"The Talent Show" - team members showcase their talents and the new team member shares their talents with the team.

"The Trivia Challenge" - team members work together to answer trivia questions related to the new team member's background and interests.

"The Group Welcome" - team members come together to formally welcome the new team member and make them feel a part of the team.

Icebreakers for a team with new leadership

Icebreakers for a team with new leadership can be an effective way to help the team get to know the new leader, as well as to help the leader get to know the team. Here are a few examples of icebreaker activities that can be used in this situation:

Introduce the leader: Have the new leader give a brief introduction of themselves, their background, and their leadership style. This will help the team get to know the leader and understand their approach to leadership.

Two Truths and a Lie: Have the new leader share three statements about themselves, two of which are true and one of which is false. The team can then guess which statement is false, helping them to learn more about the leader.

Team-building exercises: Have the team participate in team-building exercises, such as trust-building exercises, problem-solving exercises, or communication exercises. This will help the team work together more effectively and help the leader understand how the team operates.

Group Discussion: Have the team discuss about their expectations, concerns, and goals for the new leader. This will be a good opportunity to understand the team's views and to address any concerns they may have.

Idea generation: Have the leader and the team participate in an idea generation activity, such as a brainstorming session, to help the team come up with new and innovative ideas. This will help the team feel more engaged and motivated.

Getting to know you: Have the leader and the team participate in a getting-to-know-you activity, such as a speed networking session or a round-robin introduction. This will help the leader and the team get to know one another on a personal level.

"What I Bring to the Team" - Each team member shares one thing they bring to the team, such as a specific skill or experience, and how it will benefit the team.

"Leadership Style Quiz" - Team members take a quiz to determine their leadership style and then discuss their results with the new leader.

"Leadership Challenge" - The team is given a problem or challenge and must work together to solve it under the guidance of the new leader.

"Leadership Speed Dating" - Team members rotate through short one-on-one conversations with the new leader to get to know them better.

Activities that help reorganizing and welding the team

"What's in Your Bag": Team members bring in an item from their bag and have to explain why it is important to them.

"Speed Networking": Similar to speed dating, team members have short conversations with each other to learn more about one another.

"Team Building Scavenger Hunt": Team members are given a list of tasks to complete together, such as taking a group photo or finding a specific object.

"Energizer Activity": A fun, physical activity that gets team members moving and laughing, such as a game of Simon says or a dance-off.

"Collaborative Drawing": Team members work together to create a drawing or mural, with each team member contributing a specific element.

"The Amazing Race": Team members compete in a series of challenges, either in person or virtually, to complete a final task.

"Escape Room Challenge": Team members work together to solve puzzles and escape from a virtual or physical "escape room."

"The Marshmallow Challenge": Team members work together to build the tallest structure they can using only marshmallows and toothpicks.

"The Human Knot": Team members stand in a circle and grab the hand of someone who is not next to them. They then have to untangle themselves without letting go of each other's hands.

Icebreakers when a team has experienced conflict or tension

"The Apology Game" - team members take turns apologizing for past conflicts or mistakes and work on forgiveness and understanding.

"The Compliment Game" - team members take turns giving compliments to each other, building trust and positivity.

"The Empathy Walk" - team members take a walk and take turns sharing their perspective on a recent conflict or tension and actively try to understand each other's perspectives.

"The Open Discussion" - team members discuss the conflict or tension openly and actively work on finding solutions and moving forward.

"The Trust Fall" - team members work on trust and support through a trust fall exercise.

"The Forgiveness Circle" - team members sit in a circle and take turns sharing and forgiving past wrongs.

"The Communication Challenge" - team members work on communication skills and understanding through a series of exercises.

"The Conflict Resolution Game" - team members work on resolving conflicts through role-playing and problem-solving exercises.

"The Team Reflection" - team members reflect on past conflicts and tensions and work on creating a plan for moving forward and preventing similar conflicts in the future.

"The Amazing Race"

"The Amazing Race" is a team building activity that can be done outdoors. It is a fun and exciting way for teams to bond and work together to complete a series of challenges and tasks.

Example:
- Divide the team into groups of 4-6 people.
- Give each team a map of the area and a list of tasks and challenges that they need to complete.
- Tasks can include things like finding a specific landmark, solving a riddle, or taking a group photo at a certain location.
- Challenges can include things like building a shelter out of natural materials or completing a physical obstacle course.
- Set a time limit for the activity, such as 2-3 hours.
- The team that completes the most tasks and challenges within the time limit wins a prize.
- After the activity, debrief with the team to discuss what worked well and what could be improved for future team building activities.

"Team Race with a Ball"

"Team Race with a Ball" is a team building activity that can be done both outdoors and indoors. The objective of the game is for teams to work together to move a ball from one end of a course to the other, while overcoming obstacles and challenges along the way.
Example:
- Divide the team into smaller groups of 4-6 people each.
- Set up an obstacle course with a variety of challenges, such as hurdles, balance beams, and tunnels.
- Give each team a ball and a starting point.
- The teams must work together to move the ball from the starting point to the finish line, overcoming the obstacles along the way.
- The first team to reach the finish line with their ball wins.
- Variation: You could also have each team member take turns carrying the ball, or have team members race individually while carrying the ball.

This activity helps to develop teamwork, communication, and problem-solving skills, as well as encouraging creativity and resourcefulness.

"The Glass Race"

"The Glass Race" is a team building activity that can be done outdoors or in a large indoor space. The goal of the activity is for teams to race against each other while carrying a plastic glass filled with water without spilling any.

To set up the activity, divide the group into teams of 4-6 people. Give each team a plastic glass filled with water and a starting and finish line. The teams must race to the finish line while carrying the glass without spilling any water. If a team spills water, they must go back to the starting line and start again. The first team to reach the finish line without spilling any water wins.

This activity helps to build teamwork, communication, and problem-solving skills as the team members have to work together to strategize and navigate the course. It also adds an element of fun and competition to the team building experience.

ICEBREAKERS FOR MULTICULTURAL TEAMS

Activities that help to bridge cultural differences and create a more inclusive environment are important in a multicultural team because they can help to promote understanding and acceptance of different cultural perspectives. This can lead to a more cohesive team with improved communication and collaboration.

Additionally, a more inclusive environment can lead to higher job satisfaction and engagement among team members, as well as improved decision-making and problem-solving abilities.

Furthermore, it helps to reduce bias and prevent discrimination, in turn promoting a fair and equitable work environment. Overall, fostering a culture of inclusivity can be beneficial for both the team and the company as a whole.

Activities that help to bridge cultural differences and create a more inclusive environment.

Examples of team-building activities for multicultural teams:

"Cultural Mosaic": Participants share a little bit about their culture and background, including customs, traditions, and values.

"Cross-Cultural Communication": Participants role-play different scenarios where they have to communicate effectively with people from different cultures.

"Cultural Game Show": Participants compete in a game show format to test their knowledge of different cultures and customs.

"Cultural Potluck": Participants bring a dish from their culture and share it with the group, along with a brief explanation of the dish and its cultural significance.

"Cultural Book Club": Participants read a book from a culture different from their own and discuss it as a group.

"Cultural Walk": Participants take a virtual walk through different parts of the world, learning about the culture, history, and landmarks.

"Cultural Diversity Workshop": Participants attend a workshop or presentation on cultural diversity and inclusion, with a focus on understanding and respecting different cultures.

"Cross-Cultural Team Building": Participants work together on a team-building exercise that incorporates elements of different cultures, such as traditional games or activities.

"Cultural Debate": Participants debate a topic related to cultural differences and try to understand different perspectives.

"Cultural Movie Night": Participants watch a movie from a culture different from their own and discuss the cultural themes and motifs present in the film.

"Cultural Debate"

"Cultural Debate" is an activity that aims to help people understand different perspectives and bridge cultural differences. The activity is typically organized as a moderated debate on a topic related to cultural differences. The debate can be on any topic, such as cultural stereotypes, cross-cultural communication, cultural appropriation, or multiculturalism.

The debate is typically organized with teams of 2-3 people, with each team representing a different culture or perspective. Each team is given time to present their arguments, and then there is a moderated discussion where the teams can ask each other questions and respond to each other's arguments. The debate can also be organized in a round-table format where everyone participates.

The activity is beneficial in creating a more inclusive environment, as it encourages active listening, empathy, and understanding of different perspectives. It also helps to challenge stereotypes and misconceptions, and encourages people to think critically about cultural issues.

It is important to note that when conducting any activity related to cultural sensitivity, it is important to be inclusive and respectful in order to avoid any offense or hurt feelings. It's also important to have guidelines to follow and having a facilitator to moderate the debate.

"Cross-Cultural Communication"

"Cross-Cultural Communication" role play example:
Objective: To practice and improve communication skills when working with people from different cultures.
Instructions:
1. Divide the team into small groups of 4-5 people.
2. Assign each group a different culture or country to represent.
3. Provide each group with information about the customs, traditions, and communication style of their assigned culture.
4. Set up a scenario where the groups have to interact and communicate with each other, such as a business meeting or a negotiation.
5. Allow each group to prepare for the role play, giving them time to practice and develop their characters.
6. During the role play, observe and take note of any communication barriers or difficulties that arise.
7. After the role play, have a group discussion to debrief and discuss ways to improve cross-cultural communication in the future.

Benefits: This activity allows team members to gain a deeper understanding and appreciation of different cultures, as well as practice and improve communication skills in a safe and controlled environment. It also helps to identify and address any communication barriers that may arise when working with people from different backgrounds.

"Cultural Walk"

"Cultural Walk" is a team building activity that aims to promote cross-cultural understanding and appreciation. The activity can be done in-person or virtually, and it involves participants exploring different cultural spaces or neighborhoods in the local area, or learning about different cultures through online resources.

Example:

- In-Person Cultural Walk: The team is divided into small groups, each group is assigned a different cultural neighborhood or area in the city. The groups are given a map and a list of places to visit, such as cultural centers, restaurants, and shops. Each group is also given a list of questions to ask the locals and a notebook to record their observations. After exploring the area, the groups reconvene and share their experiences and observations with the rest of the team.
- Virtual Cultural Walk: The team is given a list of virtual tours, videos, and articles that highlight different cultures from around the world. Each team member is asked to choose one culture and share what they have learned with the rest of the team. The team can also use breakout rooms for small group discussions about the different cultures.

This activity helps team members understand and appreciate the cultural diversity within the team and the wider community, and can also help to improve cross-cultural communication and collaboration within the team.

ICEBREAKERS FOR DIFFERENT AGE GROUPS

When a company has a diverse workforce with a mix of employees from different age groups, it is important to use activities that help to bind these different ages together. This can help to create a more cohesive and inclusive environment, where everyone feels valued and respected. These activities can also help to break down any stereotypes or prejudices that may exist between different age groups, and foster mutual understanding and appreciation. Additionally, when age-diverse teams work together effectively, it can bring a wealth of different perspectives and ideas to the table, leading to more innovative solutions and better outcomes for the company.

This type of activities and games can also be used at employee retreats when their families are also present.

Examples of icebreakers for binding different ages together:

Here are some examples of icebreaker activities that can be used to bring different age groups together:

"Generation Mixer" where people of different ages are paired up and given prompts to discuss, such as "What was your favorite childhood toy?" or "What technology do you find most useful today?"

"Intergenerational Storytelling" where people of different ages share stories and perspectives on a shared topic, such as "Growing up in the (decade)" or "Changes in technology over time."

"Team Building Challenge" where teams are made up of people of different ages and work together to complete a task or solve a problem

"Intergenerational Debate" where different age groups debate on a topic that is relevant to all of them, such as "The Role of Social Media in Today's Society"

"Intergenerational Game Night" where people of different ages play games together, like board games or video games, and get to know each other in a fun and relaxed setting.

"Time Capsule": Have each team member bring in something that represents a significant event or memory from their past. Share and discuss the items as a team.

"Picture Puzzle": Divide the team into groups and give each group a set of pictures that represent different time periods (e.g. 1920s, 1960s, etc.). Have the team members work together to put the pictures in chronological order.

"Generation Mixer" games examples

"Generation Mixer" is a team building game that aims to bring together team members from different age groups and create a sense of understanding and respect for one another's perspectives. Here are a few examples of how this game can be played:

Example 1:
- Divide the team into groups of 4-5 people, with each group representing a different age range (e.g. 20s, 30s, 40s, 50s, 60s).
- Give each group a set of cards with questions related to their age range, such as "What was your favorite TV show growing up?" or "What was the biggest technology advancement during your teenage years?".
- Set a time limit of 10-15 minutes for each group to answer the questions and share their answers with the rest of the team.
- After the time is up, have each group present their answers to the rest of the team and encourage discussion and understanding among the different age groups.

Example 2:
- Divide the team into groups of 3-4 people, with each group representing a different generation (e.g. Baby Boomers, Gen X, Millennials, Gen Z).
- Give each group a set of cards with questions related to their generation, such as "What are some of the biggest challenges your generation has faced?" or "What are some of the most important values your generation holds?".
- Set a time limit of 20-30 minutes for each group to answer the questions and share their answers with the rest of the team.
- After the time is up, have each group present their answers to the rest of the team and encourage discussion and understanding among the different generations.

"Intergenerational Storytelling"

"Intergenerational Storytelling" is a team building activity that aims to bridge the gap between different age groups within a team. The activity can be done in-person or virtually and typically lasts for about 30-45 minutes.

Example:
1. Divide the team into small groups of 3-4 people, with each group having a mix of different age groups.
2. Each group is given a topic or theme (e.g. technology, music, fashion) and is asked to brainstorm a list of 10-15 key events or moments related to the topic that have occurred in their lifetime.
3. Each group then chooses a spokesperson to share their list with the rest of the team, giving a brief overview of the events and explaining the significance of each one.
4. As a team, discuss the similarities and differences in the experiences of the different age groups and what can be learned from them.
5. Reflect on how these differences in perspective can be used to improve communication and collaboration within the team.
6. Encourage team members to continue sharing their experiences and perspectives with one another as a way to build deeper understanding and respect for one another.

Example 3:
- Divide the team into groups of 2-3 people, with each group representing a different age range or generation.
- Give each group a set of cards with questions related to their age range or generation, such as "What is the most important lesson you have learned in your life?" or "What do you think is the biggest misconception about your age range or generation?".
- Set a time limit of 15-20 minutes for each group to answer the questions and share their answers with the rest of the team.
- After the time is up, have each group present their answers to the rest of the team and encourage discussion and understanding among the different age ranges or generations.

ICEBREAKERS FOR DIFFERENT LOCATIONS

Icebreakers for outdoor company activities

Outdoor activities can be a great way to bond with colleagues and build teamwork in a relaxed and natural setting. Outdoor can mean a terrace, the company's yard, a nearby park, not necessarily an expensive exit from the town.

Here are some examples of icebreaker activities that can be used for outdoor company activities:

"Nature Scavenger Hunt" where teams work together to find and photograph specific items in nature

"Nature Walk and Talk" where team members take a walk together and share their thoughts and ideas as they explore the outdoors

"Outdoor Obstacle Course" where teams work together to complete a series of challenges that test their problem-solving and communication skills

"Campfire Building and Storytelling" where teams work together to build a campfire and then take turns sharing stories or jokes around the fire

"Outdoor Yoga or Meditation" where team members participate in a yoga or meditation session outdoors to promote relaxation and focus.

"Geocaching Adventure" where teams use GPS to locate hidden containers filled with trinkets and logbooks, and share the items they found with each other

"Team Building Hike" where teams work together to navigate a hike, helping each other over rocky terrain and up steep inclines.

"Team Building Picnic" where teams plan and organize a picnic together and share a meal in nature.

"Outdoor Team Building Game" where teams play team building games such as Capture the flag, tug of war, or relay race

"Nature Photography Challenge" where teams have to take pictures of different objects or animals in the nature and present it to the group.

It's important to keep in mind that the activities should be tailored to the group's physical abilities, and to be mindful of the group's needs, culture, and backgrounds. It's also important to have a plan for bad weather or other unexpected situations.

"Nature Photography Challenge"

The "Nature Photography Challenge" is a fun and engaging icebreaker activity that can be used to encourage teamwork and creativity among a group of people. Here's an example of how it can be organized:

Divide the group into teams of 2-4 people.

Provide each team with a list of nature-related items or subjects that they need to photograph (e.g. a tree, a bird, a sunset, a waterfall, a flower, etc.)

Set a time limit for the challenge (e.g. 1 hour, 2 hours, etc.)

Provide each team with a camera or a smartphone.

Send the teams out into nature to photograph the items on the list.

When the time limit is up, have each team present their photographs to the group and explain the story behind each photograph and the challenges they encountered while taking it.

Encourage the group to give feedback and suggestions for improvement.

Give a prize for the team that captured the best photographs.

This activity encourages teamwork, communication, creativity, and problem-solving. It also helps team members to get to know each other better and appreciate each other's strengths and talents. It also gets them to explore and appreciate nature while getting some physical activity as well.

Outdoor activities to enhance team creativity

Outdoor activities can be an effective way to enhance team creativity, as the natural environment can provide a fresh perspective and inspiration for new ideas. Here are 10 examples of outdoor activities that can encourage creativity in teams:

Nature Scavenger Hunt: Divide the team into small groups and give them a list of items to find in the natural environment. This activity encourages exploration and problem-solving.

Outdoor Painting: Provide the team with paint, brushes, and canvas, and let them create a group painting in the outdoors. This activity encourages collaboration and creativity.

Outdoor Photography: Provide the team with cameras and let them explore the natural environment to take photographs. This activity encourages observation and creativity.

Nature Walk: Take the team on a guided nature walk to explore the natural environment and discuss how the natural world can inspire new ideas.

Outdoor Yoga: A yoga session in nature can help to focus the mind and release creativity.

Nature Writing: Give the team a writing prompt, and ask them to write a short story or poem inspired by the natural environment.

Outdoor Movie Night: Show a movie outdoors and ask the team to discuss how the story and characters relate to their work or personal lives.

"Nature Inspiration Challenge" encourage the team to find inspiration in nature and come up with new ideas related to their work.

"Creative Nature Adventure" plan a creative challenge that requires the team to think outside of the box while exploring nature.

"Nature Escape Room": Design an outdoor escape room experience that requires the team to solve puzzles and riddles in order to escape.

"Nature Escape Room"

The "Nature Escape Room" is an outdoor team building activity that encourages problem-solving, collaboration, and creativity. Here's an example of how you might set up this activity:

Create a series of puzzles and riddles that are inspired by the natural environment. For example, you might create a riddle that requires the team to find a specific tree in the park and read a message hidden in a hollowed-out branch.

Divide the team into small groups and assign each group a different puzzle or riddle to solve.

Give each group a map of the area and a set of clues to help them find the location of their puzzle or riddle.

Set a time limit for the activity, and encourage the teams to work together to solve the puzzles and riddles as quickly as possible.

Once all of the puzzles and riddles have been solved, bring the teams together for a debriefing session to discuss the challenges they faced and the lessons they learned.

As a prize, you can prepare a picnic or a dinner in the nature for the winning team.

This activity is designed to promote teamwork, communication, and creativity, and is a fun way for team members to bond and build relationships in a beautiful outdoor setting.

Icebreakers for active teams at the pool or beach

"Pool Relay Race": Divide the group into teams and have them complete a relay race in the pool, with each team member completing a different task such as swimming a lap, diving for a floating object, or carrying a noodle.

"Beach Ball Volleyball": Set up a net and play beach volleyball using a giant inflatable beach ball.

"Sunken Treasure Hunt": Hide small prizes or trinkets in the pool and have the group search for them using snorkeling gear or inner tubes.

"Floatie Race": Divide the group into teams and have them race across the pool on inflatable rafts or floaties.

"Water Balloon Toss": Divide the group into teams and have them stand on opposite sides of the pool. Have them pass water balloons back and forth, trying not to drop them.

"Pool Noodle Jousting": Divide the group into pairs and have them use pool noodles to joust against each other.

"Snorkeling Adventure": Provide snorkeling gear and take the group out to explore the ocean or a nearby reef.

"Sea Kayaking": Rent sea kayaks and take the group on a guided tour of the coastline.

"Beach Scavenger Hunt": Create a list of items to find on the beach and divide the group into teams to search for them.

"Beach Olympics": Set up a variety of games and activities on the beach such as sandcastle building, beach volleyball, or beach soccer.

"Beach Yoga": Lead the group in a yoga session on the beach.

"Sandcastle Building Competition": Divide the group into teams and have them compete to build the best sandcastle.

"Beach Frisbee Golf": Set up a course using frisbees and have the group play a round of frisbee golf.

"Beach Soccer": Set up a soccer field on the beach and have the group play a friendly game.

"Beach Volleyball": Set up a volleyball net on the beach and have the group play a game.

"Beach Bonfire": Build a bonfire on the beach and have the group roast marshmallows and tell stories around the fire.

"Beach BBQ": Cook up a barbecue on the beach and have the group enjoy a meal together.

"Beach Photography": Have the group take turns taking photos of each other on the beach.

"Beach Cleanup": Have the group spend some time cleaning up the beach and picking up litter.

"Beach Scuba Diving": Provide scuba diving equipment and take the group out to explore the ocean or a nearby reef.

Icebreakers for active teams at the mountains

Scavenger Hunt: Divide the team into small groups and provide them with a list of items to find in the mountains.

Hiking Challenge: Set a challenging hike for the team to complete together, with the goal of reaching a scenic viewpoint or summit.

Orienteering: Provide the team with maps and compasses and have them navigate through the mountains to find specific landmarks or points of interest.

Survival Challenge: Challenge the team to build shelter, start a fire, and find food using only natural materials found in the mountains.

Team Photo Challenge: Divide the team into groups and give each group a camera. They have to take creative and beautiful photos of the mountain and its surroundings.

Geocaching: Provide the team with GPS coordinates and have them search for hidden geocaches in the mountains.

Nature Walk: Have the team take a leisurely nature walk through the mountains, stopping to observe and learn about different plants and animals along the way.

Mountain Biking: Rent mountain bikes for the team and have them explore the mountains on two wheels.

Rock Climbing: Take the team rock climbing and have them work together to conquer challenging routes.

Stargazing: After a day of activities, gather the team together to stargaze and enjoy the beauty of the night sky in the mountains.

Team Building Obstacle Course: Create an obstacle course that teams have to complete together, helping each other out along the way.

Whitewater Rafting: If possible, take the team on a whitewater rafting adventure and have them work together to navigate the rapids.

Snowshoeing: Rent snowshoes for the team and have them explore the mountains during the winter months.

Campfire Building and Telling Stories: Teach the team how to build a campfire safely and have them gather around to tell stories and bond.

Zip-lining: Take the team on a zip-lining adventure and have them work together to conquer their fears.

Mountain Rescue Simulation: Run a simulated mountain rescue scenario and have the team work together to save a "stranded hiker."

Team Building Scavenger Hunt: Create a scavenger hunt that requires the team to work together to solve puzzles and complete challenges.

Photography Challenge: Give the team a set of photographs from the mountain and have them recreate them with the team.

Amazing Race: Create an "Amazing Race" style challenge that takes the team throughout the mountains, completing tasks and solving puzzles along the way.

Team Building Summit Climb: Help the team set a goal to summit a mountain together, and provide training and support to help them achieve it.

Icebreakers for active teams in the snow/ winter

Snow Scavenger Hunt: Divide teams into small groups and send them out with a list of items to find in the snow.

Snowball Volleyball: Set up a net and play a game of volleyball using snowballs instead of a regular ball.

Snowman Building Challenge: Divide teams into small groups and give them a set amount of time to build the tallest and most creative snowman.

Igloo Building Challenge: Divide teams into small groups and give them a set amount of time to build the biggest and most structurally sound igloo.

Ski or Snowboard Race: Organize a race on skis or snowboards and award prizes to the winners.

Snowshoeing Adventure: Take teams on a guided snowshoeing adventure through the mountains.

Winter Survival Challenge: Divide teams into small groups and give them a set amount of time to build a shelter and make a fire using only natural materials.

Snowy Obstacle Course: Set up a challenging obstacle course in the snow for teams to complete.

Snowball Combat: Divide teams into small groups and have them engage in a friendly snowball fight.

Hot Cocoa Challenge: Divide teams into small groups and have them compete to create the best hot cocoa recipe.

Snowy Scavenger Hunt: Divide teams into small groups and give them a list of items to find in the snow.

Winter Camping Challenge: Divide teams into small groups and give them a set amount of time to build a winter camping shelter and start a fire.

Winter Photography Challenge: Divide teams into small groups and give them a set amount of time to take the most interesting and creative winter photographs.

Ice Fishing Challenge: Organize a competition to see who can catch the most fish through a hole in the ice.

Snowy Yoga: Lead a yoga class on a snowy mountain top.

Snowmobile Adventure: Take teams on a guided snowmobile tour through the mountains.

Winter Hiking Challenge: Organize a hiking challenge through snowy mountain trails.

Sledding Competition: Divide teams into small groups and have them compete in a sledding race.

Winter Stargazing: Take teams on a guided stargazing tour in the snowy mountains.

Snowy Geocaching Adventure: Divide teams into small groups and give them a set amount of time to find geocaches hidden in the snow.

"Snowy Obstacle Course"

The "Snowy Obstacle Course" is a team building activity that can be done outdoors during the winter. It requires participants to work together to navigate through a series of obstacles while wearing snowshoes or cross-country skis. Here's an example of how this activity can be set up:

- Divide the team into groups of 4-6 people.
- Create an obstacle course that includes a series of challenges that require teamwork and communication. Some examples could include:
    - A relay race where each team member must ski or snowshoe a certain distance before passing the baton to the next person
    - A blindfolded obstacle course where one team member is blindfolded and the others guide them through a series of obstacles
    - A challenge where the team must work together to build a snow shelter
- Provide each group with a map of the obstacle course and a list of challenges they need to complete.
- Set a time limit for the course, such as 2 hours.
- At the end of the course, the team that completes the most challenges in the shortest amount of time wins a prize.
- After the course, have a debriefing session where the team can discuss their experiences and what they learned.

This activity helps team members to work together, improve communication, and problem-solving skills in a fun and challenging way. It also promotes physical activity and allows team members to bond in a unique outdoor setting.

CARD GAME OR TRIVIA ICEBREAKERS

In many of the activities that I talked about in the previous chapters, questions are also used. Like in this examples:

"Who Am I?": team members take turns giving clues about themselves, and others have to guess who they are.
"What's Your Favorite?": team members share their favorite books, movies, TV shows, etc.
"Would You Rather?": team members choose between two hypothetical scenarios.
But questions can also be used in other ways as icebreakers.

Card game or trivia icebreakers are somehow similar. There are card games to buy with ready-made team building or presentation questions, or you can write your own sets of questions on some cards and use them for team building activities.

The questions can also be used in trivia games. To use questions as an icebreaker activity, you can first divide your team into small groups or have everyone participate in a larger group discussion. Then, provide each group or individual with a list of questions. These questions can be open-ended and designed to encourage team members to share their thoughts, opinions, and experiences.

It's important to create a safe and non-judgmental space for team members to share their answers.

You can also assign a facilitator to lead the discussion and ensure that everyone has a chance to speak.

After the activity, debrief with the team and discuss any insights or connections that were made.

You can certainly adapt the questions to the specific situation for which you are organizing the icebreaks and below are several lists with useful examples:

50 Icebreaker questions to introduce or know more the team members

What's your name and where are you from?

What do you do for work or study?

What do you like to do in your free time?

What is your favorite hobby?

What is your favorite book/movie/TV show?

What is your favorite type of music?

What is your favorite food or drink?

What is your favorite vacation destination?

What is your favorite thing about your job?

What is your favorite thing about working with this team?

What is your most memorable experience?

What is something you've always wanted to try but haven't yet? What is your proudest achievement?

What is something you're currently working on?

What is a goal you're working towards?

What is a challenge you're currently facing?

What is a skill you'd like to learn?

What is a place you've always wanted to visit?

What is a tradition or custom you have in your culture?

What is a random fact about yourself?

What is your favorite quote or motto?

What is your favorite way to relax and unwind?

What is your favorite thing about yourself?

What is your favorite thing about the company?

What is your favorite thing about the team?

What is your favorite thing about the work environment?

What is your favorite thing about the team leader?

What is your favorite thing about the team culture?

What is your favorite thing about the team dynamics?

What is your favorite thing about the team's mission or vision? What is your favorite thing about the team's goals?

What is your favorite thing about the team's processes?

What is your favorite thing about the team's communication? What is your favorite thing about the team's collaboration? What is your favorite thing about the team's innovation?

What is your favorite thing about the team's work-life balance? What is your favorite thing about the team's diversity?

What is your favorite thing about the team's strengths?

What is your favorite thing about the team's challenges?

What is your favorite thing about the team's growth?

What is your favorite thing about the team's accomplishments?

What is your favorite thing about the team's opportunities?

What is your favorite thing about the team's support?

What is your favorite thing about the team's feedback?

What is your favorite thing about the team's recognition?

What is your favorite thing about the team's learning?

What is your favorite thing about the team's development?

What is your favorite thing about the team's contributions?

What is your favorite thing about the team's impact?

What is your favorite thing about the team's future?

50 Icebreaker questions to stimulate creativity in the team

What is the most creative solution you've come up with in the past?

If you could have any job in the world, what would it be?

What is the most creative project you've ever worked on?

What is something you've always wanted to create but haven't had the chance to yet?

What is something you've created that you're most proud of?

What is something you've seen or experienced that has inspired you to be more creative?

What is something you wish you were better at creating?

What is the most difficult creative challenge you've faced? What is the most unique solution you've come up with for a problem?

What is a creative hobby you have?

How do you come up with new ideas?

How do you handle creative blocks?

What is the most unusual thing you've ever created?

What is the most unconventional way you've solved a problem?

How do you decide which ideas to pursue?

What is the most innovative project you've ever worked on?

How do you measure the success of a creative project?

What is the most creative way you've marketed a product or service?

What is your favorite creative tool or resource?

What is the most creative way you've used technology?

What is the most creative way you've used data?

How do you stay motivated and engaged in a creative project?

How do you manage and prioritize multiple creative projects at once?

What is the most creative way you've used social media?

How do you handle criticism of your creative work?

How do you stay current with the latest creative trends and techniques?

What is the most creative way you've used a limited budget?

How do you brainstorm and collaborate with a team?

How do you come up with creative solutions to problems?

How do you stay creative when working under pressure?

How do you incorporate customer feedback into your creative process?

How do you stay organized and on track in a creative project?

How do you measure the ROI of a creative project?

How do you stay motivated and productive when working on a long-term creative project?

How do you balance the need for creativity with the need for efficiency in a project?

How do you stay focused and avoid distractions when working on a creative project?

How do you stay motivated and engaged when working on a project that is not your passion?

How do you use storytelling in a creative project?

How do you use humor in a creative project?

How do you use emotion in a creative project?

How do you use data visualization in a creative project?

How do you use animation in a creative project?

How do you use music in a creative project?

How do you use sound effects in a creative project?

How do you use color in a creative project?

How do you use typography in a creative project?

How do you use photography in a creative project?

How do you use video in a creative project?

How do you use web design in a creative project?

How do you use mobile design in a creative project?

50 Icebreaker Questions to help team solve their conflicts

How do you handle conflict in a team setting?

How do you approach resolving a disagreement with a team member?

Have you ever been in a situation where you had to mediate a conflict within a team? How did you handle it?

What do you think is the most common cause of conflict in a team?

How do you think a team can prevent conflicts from arising?

In your opinion, what is the best way to address a conflict within a team?

How do you think a team leader should handle conflicts within the team?

Have you ever been in a situation where you had to apologize to a team member? How did you handle it?

How do you think a team can improve its conflict resolution skills?

How do you think clear communication can help prevent conflicts within a team?

How do you think a team can learn from conflicts and use them to improve?

What are some strategies you use to stay calm and composed during a conflict?

How do you think a team can support a team member who is feeling overwhelmed by a conflict?

How do you think a team can handle conflicts that involve multiple team members?

How do you think a team can handle conflicts that involve external parties?

How do you think a team can handle conflicts that involve sensitive or confidential information?

How do you think a team can handle conflicts that involve power imbalances?

How do you think a team can handle conflicts that involve cultural or language differences?

How do you think a team can handle conflicts that involve personality clashes?

How do you think a team can handle conflicts that involve conflicting priorities?

How do you think a team can handle conflicts that involve limited resources?

How do you think a team can handle conflicts that involve different communication styles?

How do you think a team can handle conflicts that involve different working styles?

How do you think a team can handle conflicts that involve different leadership styles?

How do you think a team can handle conflicts that involve different decision-making styles?

How do you think a team can handle conflicts that involve different levels of experience or expertise?

How do you think a team can handle conflicts that involve different levels of authority or responsibility?

How do you think a team can handle conflicts that involve different levels of trust?

How do you think a team can handle conflicts that involve different levels of motivation or commitment?

How do you think a team can handle conflicts that involve different levels of accountability?

How do you think a team can handle conflicts that involve different levels of risk tolerance?

How do you think a team can handle conflicts that involve different levels of creativity or innovation?

How do you think a team can handle conflicts that involve different levels of adaptability or flexibility?

How do you think a team can handle conflicts that involve different levels of collaboration or teamwork?

How do you think a team can handle conflicts that involve different levels of customer service or satisfaction?

How do you think a team can handle conflicts that involve different levels of quality or performance?

How do you think a team can handle conflicts that involve different levels of productivity or efficiency?

How do you think a team can handle conflicts that involve different levels of cost or value?

How do you think a team can handle conflicts that involve different levels of safety or security?

How do you think a team can handle conflicts that involve different levels?

Icebreaker Questions for problem solving in the team

How do you typically approach a difficult problem or challenge?

Can you share a time when you had to think outside the box to solve a problem?

How do you prioritize and manage multiple tasks or projects at once?

How do you handle a team member who consistently disagrees with the group's decisions?

Can you share a time when you had to make a quick decision under pressure?

How do you handle a project that is not going as planned?

How do you gather and analyze information before making a decision?

How do you ensure that all team members have a say in the decision-making process?

Can you give an example of a time when you had to navigate a difficult situation with a client or customer?

How do you approach conflicts or differences of opinion within the team?

How do you handle a team member who is not pulling their weight?

How do you manage a tight deadline?

How do you encourage creativity and new ideas within the team?

How do you approach a project that is outside of your area of expertise?

How do you balance the need for quick decisions with the need for thorough research and analysis?

How do you handle difficult stakeholders?

How do you ensure that all team members are on the same page?

How do you manage changes in scope or direction for a project?

How do you identify and mitigate risks?

How do you handle a team member who is not meeting expectations?

Note that these are just examples and that you should adjust the questions to suit your team and situation. It's important to also have open discussions and encourage every team member to participate.

"How Well Do You Know Me" is a game that can be used as an icebreaker to help team members get to know each other better. The game can be played in a variety of ways, but the basic idea is that each team member will answer a set of questions about themselves, and the other team members will have to guess the answers. The questions can be about anything, such as hobbies, interests, favorite foods, etc. The team member who gets the most correct guesses wins the game. It can be a fun way to break the ice and encourage team members to open up and share more about themselves with their colleagues.

One example is:

Each team member fills out a short questionnaire about themselves, answering questions such as "What's your favorite color?", "What's your favorite hobby?", "What's your dream job?", etc.

The questionnaires are collected and shuffled, so each team member receives a questionnaire that belongs to someone else.

Team members take turns guessing who they think the questionnaire belongs to. The person who wrote the questionnaire can confirm or deny if they think the guess is correct.

The team member who correctly guesses the most questionnaires wins a prize or recognition.

This game can be fun and a great way to get team members interacting and learning more about each other, helping to build stronger relationships and a more cohesive team.

"Resolution Roulette" is a game that can be used to help a team work through conflicts and find solutions. The game uses a set of cards with different prompts or questions related to resolving conflicts. This game can be adapted to different team sizes and can be played in a variety of settings. It can be a useful tool for facilitating open communication and encouraging team members to think creatively about resolving conflicts.

Example:

This game involves a deck of cards, each with a different conflict resolution strategy written on it (e.g. "compromise," "collaboration," "mediation"). To begin the game, divide the team into smaller groups of 3-5 people. Then, have each group draw a card from the deck. The group should then discuss the scenario on the card and come up with a resolution to the conflict.

Once each group has had a chance to discuss the scenario and come up with a resolution, have the groups share their resolutions with the larger team. The other teams can then provide feedback and suggestions for how the resolution could be improved.

The game can be repeated with different scenarios, and it can be adjusted to meet the specific needs of the team. The goal of the game is to help the team learn how to effectively resolve conflicts and work together more effectively as a team. Additionally, the team can discuss afterwards how they were able to solve the conflict, what were the challenges and how they did overcome them. This can help the team to understand how they can solve similar conflicts in the future.

"The Blame Game"

"The Blame Game" is a team building activity that aims to help team members identify and address the root causes of conflicts within the team. The activity is designed to be a fun and interactive way to encourage open and honest communication among team members, as well as to promote problem-solving and collaboration. The game is played as follows:

Divide the team into small groups of 2-4 people.

Give each group a set of cards with different conflict scenarios written on them (e.g. "Two team members are not communicating effectively," "A team member is not pulling their weight," etc.).

Ask each group to select one card and discuss the scenario as a group.

After a set amount of time (e.g. 10 minutes), ask each group to present their scenario and the potential solutions they came up with to the rest of the team.

As a group, discuss the different solutions and try to identify common themes or patterns in the conflicts.

Finally, have the team brainstorm and come up with a set of guidelines or protocols for addressing and resolving conflicts in the future.

This game can be adapted to fit different team sizes and dynamics by adjusting the number of cards and scenarios, the time allocated for discussion, and the format of the presentation and debrief.

"Diversity Wheel"

"Diversity Wheel" is a card game that can be used to promote diversity and inclusion within a team. The game is played with a deck of cards, each of which has a different question related to diversity and inclusion. The questions can be about personal experiences, cultural backgrounds, or perspectives on diversity and inclusion.

To play, the team is divided into small groups of 3-5 people.

Each group receives a deck of cards and takes turns picking a card from the deck and answering the question on the card. The goal of the game is for team members to learn more about each other's diverse backgrounds, experiences and perspectives. The game can be adapted to suit the size and needs of the team.

Example question cards:

What is your cultural background?

What is your most memorable experience related to diversity and inclusion?

How do you think diversity and inclusion can benefit our team?

How do you define diversity?

What steps do you think we should take to create a more inclusive team environment?

This game can be a great way to encourage open and honest conversations about diversity and inclusion within a team, and help team members understand and appreciate each other's perspectives.

Card games templates to print

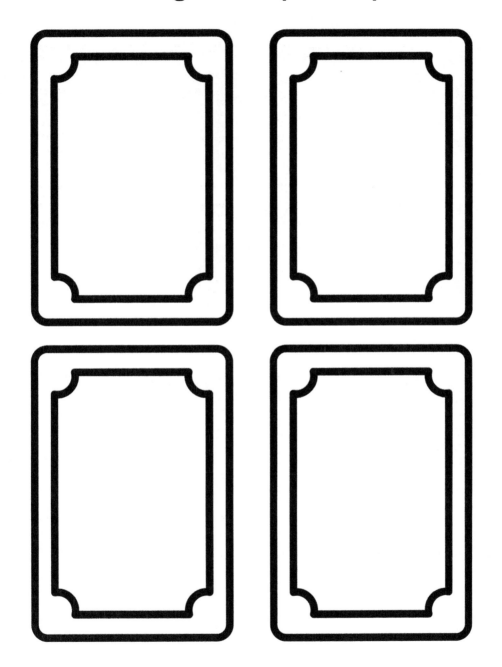

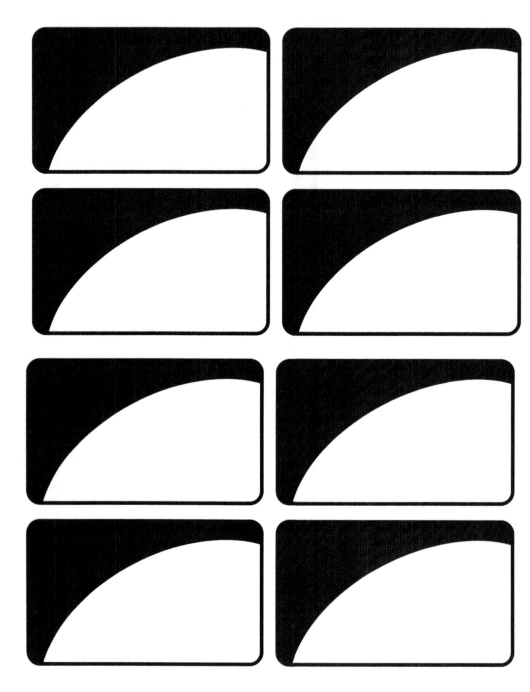

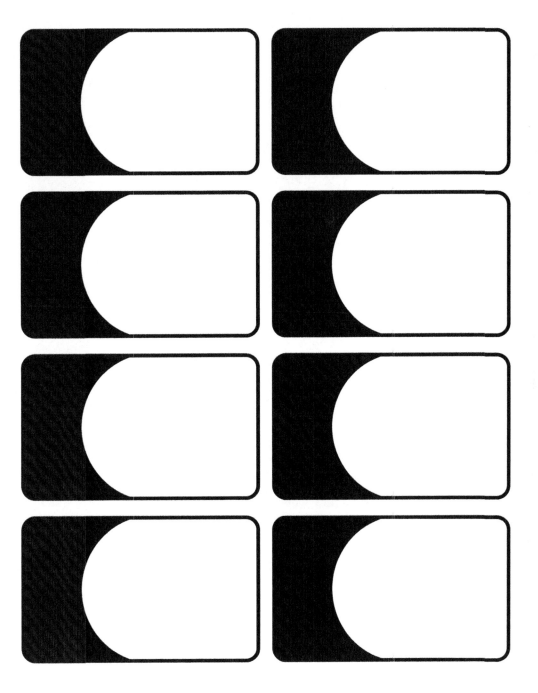

Thank You

Thank you for purchasing "My Big Book of Ice Breakers and Games for Meetings"! We hope that this book will be a valuable resource for you as you work to improve team dynamics and communication within your organization.

Inside this book, you'll find a variety of ice breaker activities and games that are designed to help people get to know each other better, work together more effectively, and build stronger teams. Whether you're looking for ways to improve team cohesion, promote creativity and innovation, or simply create a more inclusive and welcoming environment, you'll find plenty of ideas and inspiration in these pages.

We've also included tips and advice on how to adapt these activities to different team sizes and settings, so you can make the most of the resources in this book no matter what type of team you're working with.

So go ahead and dive in! And if you have any questions or feedback, please don't hesitate to reach out to us at romediaweb@gmail.com . We'd love to hear from you.

Once again, thank you for your purchase, and we hope you enjoy using this book to build stronger, more cohesive teams.

Sincerely,

Rogers T

Theodora Rogers

Printed in Great Britain
by Amazon